TEACHER'S GUIDE

# The Story of Ferdinand

by Munro Leaf

DSC Partner Unit for Puffin Books Edition, 1977
Suggested Grade Range 1–2

## Child Development Project
**READING, THINKING & CARING**

CHILD DEVELOPMENT PROJECT

Developmental Studies Center
2000 Embarcadero, Suite 305
Oakland, CA 94606
510-533-0213

Copyright © 1996
Developmental Studies Center

ACKNOWLEDGMENTS

[1] 1991 by Celeste West and Booklegger Publishing for "You Say" by Elsa Gidlow from *Mother Gave a Shout*, edited by Susanna Steele and Morag Styles, Volcano Press, 1991. Reprinted by permission of Booklegger Publishing, 555 29th Street, San Francisco, CA 94131.

[2] 1975 by American Universal Artforms Corp. for "Getting to Know Me" by Libby Stopple from *A Box of Peppermints*, American Universal Artforms, 1975.

ISBN 1-885603-93-2

Teacher's Guide

# The Story of Ferdinand

**BACKGROUND FOR THE TEACHER**
Synopsis ... 1
Things students need to know ... 1
Vocabulary development ... 2
Ideas suggested by the story ... 2
Related books ... 2

**INTRODUCTORY ACTIVITIES**
You Say ... 4
A Special Place ... 4
Ferdinand's Bouquet ... 4
Doing What I Want ... 5

**PARTNER READING** ... 5
**PARTNER PAGES**
Reading 1 ... 7
Reading 2 ... 8

**CONNECTION ACTIVITIES**
Getting to Know Me ... 9
Mother and Son ... 9
Illustration Narration ... 10
Father Ferdinand ... 10
Times When I Was Different ... 10
Favorite Words ... 10
I Like Being Alone ... 10
I'm Feeling . . . ... 11

**HOME ACTIVITY**
Being Different ... 13

**ACTIVIDAD FAMILIAR**
El ser distinto ... 15

# Background for the Teacher

The following information is provided to highlight the unit's themes and any background knowledge or vocabulary work that may be indicated for students. Two sections, SYNOPSIS and IDEAS SUGGESTED BY THE STORY, are intended only for the teacher, as a help in anticipating issues students might raise about the story. However, students may enjoy brainstorming their *own* list of IDEAS SUGGESTED BY THE STORY as a closure activity. The final background section, RELATED BOOKS, addresses some of the themes in *The Story of Ferdinand* and provides a source for further reading.

## Synopsis

While all of the other bulls delight in fighting and butting heads, Ferdinand loves just to sit and smell the flowers. His wise and understanding mother recognizes and supports his individuality. Ferdinand's tranquility is threatened when he is chosen for a bullfight—but his disinterest in fighting proves unshakable, and he retires, happily, to pasture.

## Things students need to know

**Spain and Madrid.** Help students locate Spain on a map or globe. Tell students this is where *The Story of Ferdinand* takes place. Then help them locate Madrid, where the bullfight in the story occurs, and tell them that this is the biggest city in Spain.

**Bullfighting.** Tell students that bullfighting is a sport in some countries. People come to a big arena to watch a bull and a man try to kill each other.

**Cork Trees.** Tell students that the bark from cork trees is used to make corks (you might bring a few corks as examples). The bark of a cork tree feels just like a finished cork, making a cork tree quite comfortable to sit against. A couple of the illustrations show corks growing on the tree—once the students have read the story a few times, or if a child asks about this, explain that this is just an example of the illustrator's sense of humor.

## Vocabulary development

Write the bullfight-related words (*banderilleros, picadores, matador*) on the board and pronounce them a few times with the students (each is explained in the book as soon as it appears).

Other words students may need help pronouncing include *pasture, roughest, fierce,* and *sword*.

## Ideas suggested by the story

- ❏ It is okay to be different.

- ❏ Different things are pleasing to different people (and to different bulls).

- ❏ Being by yourself is not the same as being lonesome.

- ❏ It is important for children to have a parent or other adult who understands what makes them special.

- ❏ Sometimes it takes strength of character not to fight.

- ❏ First impressions can be wrong.

## Related books

Lewis, Marjorie  **Ernie and the Mile-Long Muffler**
*Coward, McCann & Geoghegan, 1982*
While recovering from the chicken pox, Ernie decides to get into a book of world records by knitting a mile-long muffler. When the boys in Ernie's fourth-grade class see him knitting, he becomes the butt of their jokes. Gradually, however, everyone in the class learns to knit and gets involved in Ernie's project.

| | |
|---|---|
| Lionni, Leo | **Frederick**<br>*Pantheon, 1966*<br>Unlike the other mice, Frederick is a dreamer. Not until the dark days of winter do the other mice stop taunting Frederick and learn to appreciate his ability to dream. |
| Lionni, Leo | **Swimmy**<br>*Pantheon, 1963*<br>Swimmy is black; all the other little fish are red. When the big fish threaten, Swimmy thinks of a way that they can all work together to be free and safe. |
| Schulman, Janet | **Jenny and the Tennis Nut**<br>*Greenwillow Books, 1978*<br>Jenny's father has dreams of her becoming a great tennis player, while she dreams of becoming a great circus acrobat. Eventually her father learns to appreciate that Jenny's game is turning cartwheels and doing flips. |
| Zolotow, Charlotte | **William's Doll**<br>*Harper & Row, 1972*<br>William wants a doll of his own to cuddle and care for, in spite of his brother's and a neighbor boy's ridicule. His father keeps giving him other things, which are fine but "have nothing to do with the doll." Finally William's grandmother fulfills his wish and convinces his father of its importance. |

# Introductory Activities

From the activities below, select one or two that are best suited to your class.

## Suggestions for introducing the story

**You Say.** Write the poem below on the chalkboard. Read it to the class twice. Make sure students understand what *mysterious* and *faithful* mean. Then have students in groups of four discuss how they might describe someone who can be "faithful to apples" in "a land of oranges."

*You Say*

You say I am mysterious.
Let me explain myself:
In a land of oranges
I am faithful to apples.

—*Elsa Gidlow*[1]

**A Special Place.** Tell the students that the main character in this story, Ferdinand, has a special place he likes to go where he is happy being alone (you might show them the picture of young Ferdinand sitting under the cork tree). Have partners interview each other about a special place they like to go and how they feel there. Then have partners draw each other's special place. (A variation of this might be to have students interview each other about their favorite spots on the playground.)

**Ferdinand's Bouquet.** Bring a fragrant bunch of flowers to class. In the morning ask that each child smell the flowers sometime during that day. The next day have them discuss how they felt about smelling the flowers. (They won't all enjoy it. Not everyone is a Ferdinand!) Discuss how we often like different things. Why is the world more interesting because of diversity?

DSC PARTNER UNIT

**Doing What I Want.** Tell the students about a time when you did something you wanted to do even though everyone else (friends, classmates, or some other such group) was doing something else. Emphasize your having made an individual choice and being happy with that rather than any conflict that may have arisen from having made that choice. Then ask the children to recall a time when they did not want to do what all of the other children were doing and were happy with what they chose to do instead. Invite volunteers to describe their choices for the class.

# Partner Reading

Before students read the book to each other, read the story aloud once to the class. Students may or may not wish to follow along as you read. This reading can immediately precede students reading to each other, and it need not be followed by any discussion.

# Partner Pages

**Reading 1**  Take turns, by pages, reading the story to each other. Take time to enjoy the pictures!

**Partner Discussion.** After you have read the story to each other, talk with your partner about this question:

**Why do you think Ferdinand enjoyed smelling the flowers more than butting heads and fighting?**

**Reading 2** Take turns reading the story to each other again. This time read different pages than you read before.

**Partner Activity.** After you have read the story to each other, talk with your partner about what you might like or not like about Ferdinand. Then complete the following chart:

|  | Like about Ferdinand | Don't Like about Ferdinand |
|---|---|---|
| Both of Us |  |  |
| One of Us |  |  |

# Connection Activities

When students have completed the book and partner activities, bring the class back together for one or two of the activities below.

**Connections—for the whole class**

**Getting to Know Me.** Write the poem below on the board. Read it aloud once, and then have partners read it together. Have partners, and then the whole class, discuss the following question:

**How might this poem make Ferdinand feel?**

*Getting to Know Me*

Sometimes
I sit under that old tree
On the vacant lot . . .
The one that has the long limb
That rocks when the wind
Blows.

That way I can curl up
All by myself
And know I'm
Still
Me.

—*Libby Stopple*[2]

**Mother and Son.** Have the class discuss what they like or don't like about Ferdinand's mother. You might have them consider the following question:

**What does it mean to be an "understanding" mother?**

After the class has discussed what they think about Ferdinand's mother, have partners practice a role-play about what Ferdinand might tell his mother when he got back from Madrid, and what his mother might say.

**Illustration Narration.** Cut up an extra copy of or photocopy the illustrations from *The Story of Ferdinand* (all except for the title page and "The End" page); you will have 34 pictures. Put white tape or correction fluid over the text on the first and last illustrations. Mount the pictures and give one to each child. Have students study their picture and think about the part of the story it tells. Have students tell their part in their own words.

## Connections—for students working in pairs

**Father Ferdinand.** Have partners tell each other what kind of father they think Ferdinand would be. Have them discuss why they would or would not want to have Ferdinand for a father.

**Times When I Was Different.** Have partners tell each other about a person (or people) who encouraged them to do something even though it was different from what the rest of the crowd was doing. Have them talk about how they felt about being encouraged by that special person.

**Favorite Words.** Have partners make a list of their favorite words that they read in the story.

## Connections—for students working individually

**I Like Being Alone.** Most people like being alone sometimes. Ask each student to make a list of what he or she likes doing alone.

For example, here is one child's list:

> I like being alone so I can run as fast as I want.
> I like being alone so I can watch my TV program.
> I like being alone so I don't have to worry about sharing.
> I like being alone so I can talk to myself.
> I like being alone so I don't have to follow orders.
> I like being alone so I can sing all I want.

**I'm Feeling . . .** Give each child one of the mounted pictures (see "Illustration Narration" activity above). Ask students to study their pictures carefully. Have them choose one character in their picture (some of the pictures show only one character) and then tell a partner a little about what that character is feeling or thinking in that picture. Have them write how they feel as that character.

For example:

> *Ferdinand's Mother*
> I used to worry about my son. I thought he might be lonesome. He says he's happy smelling flowers. I want him to do what he wants. I like having a son who is peaceful. I love him.

## Connections—for a home activity

**Being Different.** Remind the class of the ways they have already talked about how different people like to do different things. Then tell students you want them to ask a parent or other adult about some of the favorite (and perhaps unusual) things that the adult liked to do as a child.

**HOME ACTIVITY**

# Being Different

**Dear Family Member or Family Friend,**

In class we have been reading *The Story of Ferdinand,* by Munro Leaf, a tale of a bull who likes to "sit just quietly and smell the flowers" rather than run and play with the other bulls. Ferdinand doesn't mind that he is different, because he does what makes him happy.

For this activity, please tell your child about some of the favorite (and perhaps unusual) things that you liked to do as a child. On the back of this sheet have your child draw a picture of you doing this favorite thing as a child. Then help your child write a caption for this picture.

Thanks for your time, and have fun!

**Activity Starters**

In the space below, list some of your favorite childhood activities. From this list choose one to talk about in greater detail with your child.

**Drawing Activity:** Have your child draw a picture of one of the childhood activities you talked about. Help your child write a caption for this picture.

**Comments:** After you have completed this activity, each of you please sign your name and the date at the bottom of the page. If you have any comments about the activity, please write them in the space below.

*Signatures*                                *Date*

_____      _____

_____

*Please have your child return this activity to school. Thank you.*

## ACTIVIDAD FAMILIAR

# El ser distinto

**Estimados padres, familiares o amigos:**

En la clase estamos leyendo *The Story of Ferdinand* (*El cuento de Ferdinando*), por Munro Leaf. Este cuento trata de un toro que prefiere "sentarse tranquilo a oler las flores" en lugar de correr y jugar con los otros toros. A Ferdinando no le importa ser distinto, porque hace lo que le trae satisfacción y felicidad.

Para esta actividad, haga el favor de contarle a su hijo o hija sobre algunas de las actividades favoritas (y quizá poco comunes) que le entretenían cuando era menor. En el revés de la página, invite a su hijo o hija a hacer un dibujo de usted llevando a cabo esa actividad cuando era menor. Luego ayúdele a escribir un titular para su dibujo.

Gracias por su atención, y ¡diviértanse!

**Indicaciones para comenzar la actividad**

En el espacio que sigue, escriba una lista de algunas de sus actividades favoritas de cuando era niño o niña. Luego escoja una de estas actividades para hablar sobre ella más detalladamente con su hijo o hija.

**Actividad de dibujo:** Invite a su hijo o hija a hacer un dibujo de una de las actividades de las que han conversado. Ayúdele a su hijo o hija a escribir un titular para su dibujo.

**Comentarios:** Después de completar esta actividad, por favor firmen ambos al pie de la página y escriban la fecha. Si tiene cualquier comentario sobre la actividad, favor de escribirlo aquí.

*Firmas*  *Fecha*

_____  _____

_____

*Haga el favor de devolver esta hoja a la escuela con su hijo o hija. Muchísimas gracias.*

DSC PARTNER UNIT

# The Literature Project
## READING FOR REAL

# Island of the Blue Dolphins
by Scott O'Dell

*DSC Partner Unit for Dell Yearling Edition, 1987*

*Suggested Grade Range 5–7*

TEACHER'S GUIDE

THE LITERATURE PROJECT

DEVELOPMENTAL STUDIES CENTER
2000 EMBARCADERO, SUITE 305
OAKLAND, CA 94606
(510) 533-0213

COPYRIGHT © 1996
DEVELOPMENTAL STUDIES
CENTER

ACKNOWLEDGMENTS

[1] "Loneliness" by Felice Holman from *I Like You If You Like Me*, edited by Myra Cohn Livingston. Permission of Felice Holman, copyright owner.
[2] 1966 by Mary O'Neill for "The Wonderful Words" in *Words Words Words*, Doubleday & Co., Inc., 1966. Used by permission of Doubleday, a division of Bantam Doubleday Dell Publishing Group, Inc.

ISBN 1-885603-18-5

# Teacher's Guide
# Island of the Blue Dolphins

| | | |
|---|---|---|
| **BACKGROUND FOR THE TEACHER** | | |
| Synopsis | 1 | |
| Things Students Need to Know | 1 | |
| Vocabulary Development | 2 | |
| Difficult Word List | 3 | |
| Ideas Suggested by the Story | 4 | |
| Related Books | 5 | |
| | | |
| **INTRODUCTORY ACTIVITIES** | | |
| Questions to Karana | 6 | |
| *class activity* | | |
| Loneliness | 6 | |
| *poem discussion* | | |
| Scavenging from Nature | 7 | |
| *class activity* | | |
| Feathers | 7 | |
| *class activity* | | |
| | | |
| **PARTNER READING AND RELATED ACTIVITIES** | | |
| **PARTNER PAGES** | | |
| Reading 1 (pp. 1–14) | pp1 | |
| *partner activity* | | |
| Reading 2 (pp. 15–24) | pp3 | |
| *partner activity* | | |
| Reading 3 (pp. 25–40) | pp3 | |
| *partner discussion* | | |
| Reading 4 (pp. 41–58) | pp4 | |
| *partner discussion* | | |
| Reading 5 (pp. 59–68) | pp4 | |
| *partner discussion* | | |
| Reading 6 (pp. 69–79) | pp5 | |
| *partner activity* | | |
| Reading 7 (pp. 80–90) | pp5 | |
| *partner discussion* | | |
| Reading 8 (pp. 91–104) | pp6 | |
| *partner activity* | | |

| | | |
|---|---|---|
| Reading 9 (pp. 105–124) | 16 | |
| *partner discussion* | | |
| Reading 10 (pp. 125–140) | pp7 | |
| *partner discussion* | | |
| Reading 11 (pp. 141–146) | pp7 | |
| *partner discussion* | | |
| Reading 12 (pp. 147–156) | pp7 | |
| *partner activity* | | |
| Reading 13 (pp. 157–160) | pp7 | |
| *something to think about* | | |
| Reading 14 (pp. 161–170) | pp8 | |
| *partner discussion* | | |
| Reading 15 (pp. 171–181) | pp8 | |
| *partner activity* | | |
| Reading 16 (pp. 182–184) | pp8 | |
| *partner discussion* | | |
| Looking Back | pp9 | |
| *partner discussion, individual review art activities* | | |
| | | |
| **CONNECTION ACTIVITIES** | | |
| Wonderful Words I | 9 | |
| *poem discussion* | | |
| Wonderful Words II | 10 | |
| *small-group activity* | | |
| Island Images | 10 | |
| *small-group activity* | | |
| Preserving the Past | 10 | |
| *small-group activity* | | |
| A Monument for Karana | 10 | |
| *art activity* | | |
| HOME ACTIVITY | | |
| Society's Rules | 10 | |